Surayya's Story

Author: Kim Robinson

Illustrated By: Joanne David

My name is Surayya

I have eyes bright as fire

I was born tiny, and everyday
I get higher

My mommy is Lina

My Daddy is Khalil

I play with my grandparents
While mommy and daddy work

My uncle C. J. loves to babysit
me on weekends.

While my aunt Natalie takes care of
my diapers and meals

I will be walking soon

I am learning to use a spoon

I can drink from a straw

But when I am tired I prefer my ba ba

I am talking in my own language

Grownups are always trying to translate everything I say.

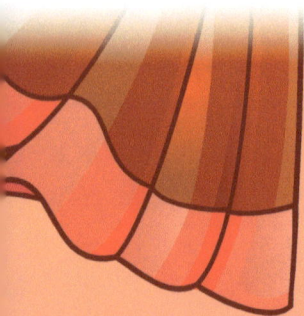

Though they are usually wrong

I love that they try anyway

When we go somewhere I have a car seat

When it is time to eat I have a high chair

I have a play pen where I hang out with my friends.

I love swimming in the tub.

Grandma and granddad take me to the pool

I call my grandfather pop pop

My mommy and daddy are beautiful parents

Grandma and pop pop love to hold me

I Love riding in my chair

I had almost given up on becoming a grandmother. Then my daughter announced that she was pregnant. I was overjoyed and called all of my friends who had grandchildren, many of whom had even had great-grandchildren.

They all welcomed me to the grandmother's club.

I am excited to share this journey with you through this series.

Kim Robinson

www.ingramcontent.com/pod-product-compliance
Lightning Source LLC
Chambersburg PA
CBHW041428090426

42741CB00002B/84